re-using & recycling

Rubber

Ruth Thomson

Photography by Neil Thomson

W

FRANKLIN WATTS
LONDON • SYDNEY

First published in 2006 by
Franklin Watts
338 Euston Road
London NW1 3BH

Franklin Watts Australia
Hachette Children's Books
Level 17/207 Kent Street
Sydney NSW 2000

Editor: Rachel Cooke
Design: Holly Mann
Art Director: Rachel Hamdi

Additional photography
Thanks are due to the following for kind
permission to reproduce photographs:
Franklin Watts 4/5, 6tl, 6tr, 6bl, 7tr, 9tr, 9cl,
9bl, 9br, 21tr; JCB 7tl; Continental 8tr, 8bl;
Ecoscene/Christine Osborne 9l; Environment
Agency UK 11bl; Earthship Inc. 12, 13;
Agripicture Images 24; Playtop 27.

ISBN 0 7496 6104 6

A CIP catalogue record for this book is
available from the British Library.

Dewey Decimal Classification Number: 678'.2

Printed in China

Acknowledgements
The author and publisher wish to thank the
following people for their help with this book:
Paul Dodo and Fungile Mtata (Aquatrap);
Mathapelo Ngaka and Zandi Maishe
(Monkeybiz); Karen Jacobsen (Earthship Inc.);
Braam and Daleen Muller (NUTU); Mncedisi
Mbundu; Playtop; Dev (Karm Marg/Jugaad);
Osama Ali, Sue Adler and Mark Watson.

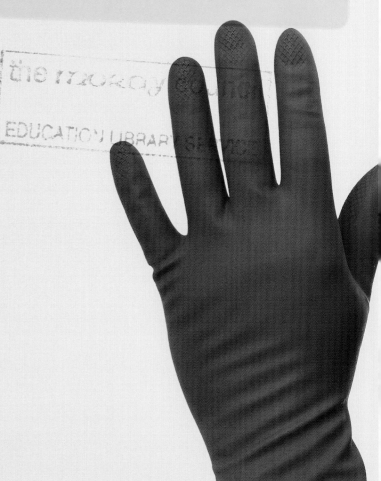

Contents

Words printed in **bold** are explained in the glossary

What is rubber like?

Rubber is an unusual **material** which bends, stretches and bounces.

Rubber is elastic.
When you pull a rubber band it stretches. When you let go it springs back into shape.

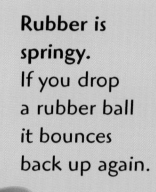

Rubber is springy.
If you drop a rubber ball it bounces back up again.

Rubber is air-tight.
When you blow up a rubber balloon, it holds air inside.

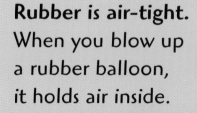

Rubber has a soft surface
which grips well.
Rubber tyres do not slip
on soft, muddy ground.

Rubber is **waterproof.**
When water falls on rubber
it does not soak in. Rubber boots
keep your feet dry on wet ground.

Boing! Boing!
Sports such as tennis
and basketball are
played with rubber balls.

Making rubber

Natural rubber is made from **latex**. This is the sticky white **sap** found under the bark of the tall rubber tree.

Rubber trees

Rubber trees are grown in **plantations** in warm, wet countries near the **Equator**. Most plantations are in Malaysia, Indonesia and Thailand.

Rubber trees grow in rows.

The tappers tap each tree every few days.

Collecting the latex

Plantation workers, known as **tappers**, cut a slanting slit in the tree bark and attach a spout and a small cup underneath. The latex runs down the groove into the cup. The latex has tiny bits of rubber in it.

Separating the rubber

Workers tip the latex into a tank and add **acid**. This makes the rubber bits clump together into solid lumps.

Rolling the rubber

The rubber clumps pass through rollers, which squeeze out all the water and roll the clumps into flat sheets. These are hung on racks to dry.

Sheets of rubber drying

The rubber is sent to **factories** all over the world, where it is shaped into all sorts of things.

IT'S A FACT

Not all rubber is natural. Most rubber is now made in factories with chemicals made from **oil**. This is called **synthetic** rubber.

LOOK AND SEE

Look around your home to see how many everyday things are made with rubber.

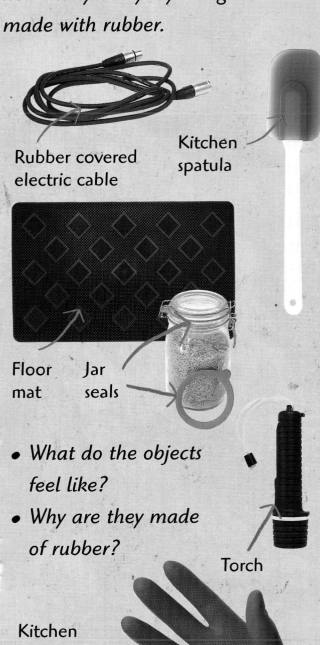

Rubber covered electric cable

Kitchen spatula

Floor mat

Jar seals

Torch

- *What do the objects feel like?*
- *Why are they made of rubber?*

Kitchen gloves (made of latex)

9

Tons of tyres

Cars and trucks have rubber tyres with a pattern of grooves and ridges, called the tread. The tread helps tyres grip the road, even when it is wet. When the tread becomes smooth, tyres are worn out.

Throwing away tyres

It is not easy to get rid of old tyres. Rubber does not **rot** if it is buried. Burning rubber can produce harmful **gases** and thick smoke. Piling tyres in a dump is a fire risk and offers shelter for **pests**, such as rats. The tyres hold water and can be a breeding ground for mosquitoes.

Re-using old tyres

Old tyres are so strong, heavy and springy, they can be **re-used** in all sorts of places.

Tyres often hang along harbour walls and over the sides of ships. They protect both the ships and the walls from damage.

Bulky barriers

Go-kart circuits and bike tracks are often lined with safety barriers made of tyres.

Embankments and walls

Tyre **bales** make good **embankments** against floods. Each one is made from 100 used tyres squashed and tied together.

Walls made of used tyres tied together with rope or wire can help prevent soil **erosion** on soft, crumbly hillsides.

Heavy weights

Farmers use tyres as weights to hold down plastic sheeting over their cut grass. The grass turns into **silage** that cows will feed on in winter.

Extraordinary earthships

Michael Reynolds, an American architect, designs houses that people can build themselves using waste tyres and drink cans. He calls these houses 'earthships'.

Each tyre is laid in place and rammed tightly with earth to make a building block.

Harnessing nature

Earthships use the powers of nature. They are heated by the sun and catch water from rain and snow. They make their own electricity from **solar** and wind energy, process their own **sewage** and have a greenhouse for growing food.

The tyres are arranged in staggered lines, just like clay bricks, to make the walls.

Solid walls

The earthships have a row of U-shaped rooms. Each room has three solid tyre walls. These are covered with mud and plaster to a smooth finish. The front wall has glass panels to trap the energy from the sun.

Empty aluminium drink cans make good fillers for walls that do not bear any weight.

The greenhouse hallway gets light all day. It is a good place to grow plants.

The thick, heavy walls of the rooms behind the hallway store heat by day and slowly release it by night.

The floor is made of smooth **adobe**.

The windows are made of two layers of glass (double-glazed). This helps trap heat.

The wooden beams are made from local trees.

Tyre transformations

People have transformed tyres into unusual things.

Pretty planters

1. This South African cuts off one side of tyres to make planters. Here, he is painting the outside of one.

2. He glues plastic mesh across the base of the planter. This lets water drain out when the planter is filled with soil and flowers.

3. He sells the planters by the roadside to passing drivers.

Comfortable swings

Tyres can be cut to make swings.

The curved shape of the tyre makes a perfect seat.

A clever climbing frame

Rows of old tyres make rungs for this climbing frame in India.

A tower for trees

A tower of tyres protects this young tree from damage, but gives it plenty of room to grow.

Rescued rubber

In some places, people cut old tyres into pieces and craft the rubber into useful new objects.

Tyre treasures

In Morocco, there are workshops that specialise in making buckets and water containers from old tyres.

Builders use the buckets for carrying rubble or bricks.

People use the buckets at home for holding wood or tools.

Donkey owners use the buckets for feeding their animals.

Careful cutting

This man is using a very sharp knife to cut and slice tyres into thin strips.

Shaping the strips

He cuts the strips into pieces. He glues and nails them together to make objects like these.

Picture frame

Container

Water bottle

Bridles and blinkers

Donkeys sometimes wear bridles and blinkers made of re-used scraps of rubber. The rubber is comfortable for them to wear. It is also far cheaper than leather.

Rubber shoes

Shoes often have rubber soles and heels. The springy rubber soaks up the shock of your footsteps on hard ground and makes walking more comfortable.

In countries where shoes are expensive, cobblers make cheap, hard-wearing shoes with rubber from old tyres.

Rubber sole   Rubber heel

Sturdy sandals

In South Africa, cobblers make sandals entirely from rubber. They use white-walled tyres from vans and cut patterns into the rubber.

Soft slippers

In Morocco, there is a long tradition of making soft slippers with leather uppers and soles. Now, some shoemakers make these slippers with tougher scrap rubber soles.

Bath shoes

In Egypt, people wear shoes for bathing before they go to prayers in a mosque. This cobbler makes shoes from wood and scrap rubber, which will not rot when they get wet.

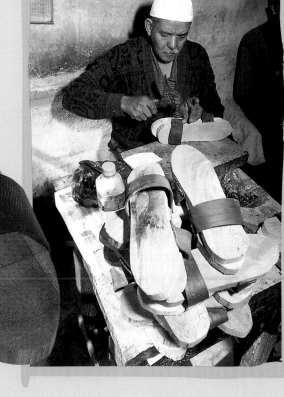

Inner tube inventions

People make unexpected things with discarded rubber **inner tubes**. It is easy to cut these soft tubes with scissors.

Fancy footwork

Children play in the narrow alleys of towns in Morocco. Instead of using a ball, they make a bundle of inner tube strips tied tightly together. They try to keep the bundle up in the air for as long as possible.

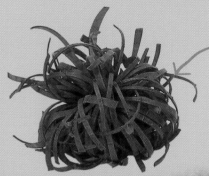

Bundle of tied-up rubber strips

Tyres for toys

In parts of Africa, craftsmen make toy bikes, trucks and cars from scrap metal and wire. They wind strips of inner tube around the wheels to make the tyres.

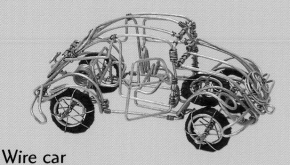

Wire car

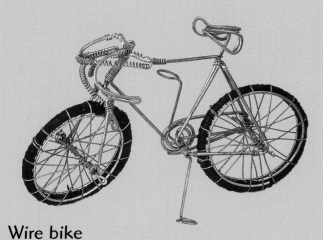

Wire bike

Scrap metal jeep

- *If you have a bicycle, keep the tyres well inflated so that they last longer.*

- *Learn how to mend the inner tube if you get a puncture.*

In countries where inner tubes are expensive, people patch them over and over again, like this.

Remarkable rubber

Inventive designers are re-using inner tubes to make fashion accessories.

Beads and bracelets

In South Africa, craftswomen make bracelets with rubber beads or plaited rubber strips.

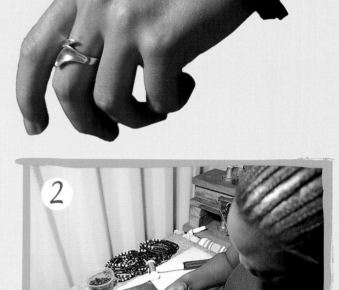

1. To make beads, they punch circles of rubber out of discarded truck inner tubes.

2. They punch holes in the circles to turn them into beads.

3. They string the beads together on a strip of rubber and finish the bracelet off with a rubber clasp.

Plaited rubber bracelets

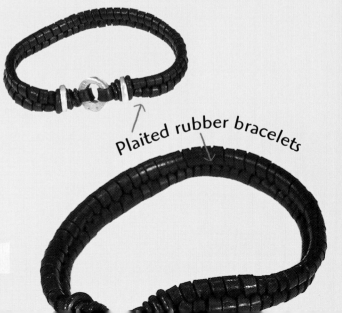

22

You're framed

Bands of inner tube, joined with knotted rubber strips and washers, make a sturdy picture frame.

Phone protector

This rubber mobile phone holder protects a phone from knocks and bumps.

Numbered bags

In South Africa, when people move towns, they have to change their car number plates. A clever car salesman had the idea of joining discarded number plates with a piece of inner tube to make unique handbags like this one.

Rubber remnants

Since rubber is tough and waterproof,
it is a perfect material to re-use outside.

A soft surface

Tyres are chopped into small
pieces and mixed with sand
for horse arenas.

The surface is comfortable for
horses. It also protects riders
from injury if they fall off.

A water trap

In countries with scarce rain and sandy soil, it is hard for plants to grow. Old tyres and inner tubes are ideal for making water traps.

Water trap

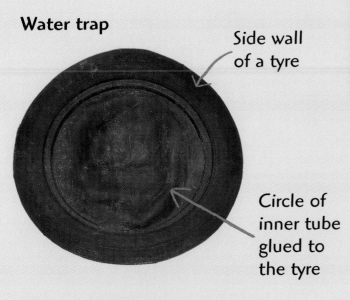

Side wall of a tyre

Circle of inner tube glued to the tyre

This water trap has been left uncovered to show how well it holds water. Gaps between water traps let some water drain away, so the land does not become too wet.

People dig a trench in the ground and lay water traps in rows. Then they cover the traps with soil and sow seeds.

Plants that grow on top of water traps grow far better than those without this extra water supply.

Recycling rubber

Millions of scrap truck tyres are **recycled** into tiny granules called rubber crumb. These can be bonded together to make a new material.

Surprising stationery

Notebook covers and pencil cases made from recycled rubber are very hard-wearing.

Notebook

USED TO BE A CAR TYRE...

Pencil case

A mouse mat

The rubber surface is smooth enough to use as a mat for a computer mouse.

Mouse mat

Finely shredded

Tyres are fed through several grinders with sharp blades. Each one in turn chops the rubber into smaller and smaller pieces.

A safe surface

The recycled rubber bits are glued together into
a thick layer. This is laid under new playground surfaces.
If children fall over, they are less likely to hurt themselves.

Glossary

acid a sort of chemical

adobe a mixture of mud and straw

bale a large bundle

bonded joined together firmly

embankment a steep bank or mound built up to keep water within a certain place

Equator the imaginary line around the centre of the Earth, halfway between the North and South Poles

erosion the gradual wearing away of something, such as soil or rock

factory a building where things are made in large numbers using machines

gas a substance that is neither a solid nor a liquid. Air is a mixture of gases

inner tube the hollow tube inside a tyre, which is filled with air

latex the milky sap of the rubber tree

material a substance used to make something else

natural found in the world, not made by people or machines

oil a sticky, black liquid found under the ground or sea

pest an insect or animal that eats crops or destroys things

plantation a large area of land used for growing only one type of plant, such as rubber trees, tea, coffee or bananas

recycle to use an existing object or material to make something new

re-use to use again

rot the natural way a material slowly breaks down into lots of smaller, different substances

sap the liquid that carries food around a plant

sewage the waste from toilets in buildings

silage green fodder for animals that is stored for winter feed

solar powered by energy from the sun

synthetic not natural; made by people

tapper someone who slits the bark of a rubber tree to let the latex flow out

waterproof not letting water in or out

Guess what?

- Nearly 80% of the world's natural rubber is grown in just three countries – Malaysia, Indonesia and Thailand.

- More than two thirds of all rubber produced is used to make tyres for cars, trucks, tractors and aeroplanes.

- Most cars use 17 tyres in their lifetime.

- Tyre dumps often catch fire. These are almost impossible to put out and can burn for weeks. They poison the soil and the water and pollute the air.

- Every day in the UK more than 100,000 worn-out tyres are taken off cars, vans and trucks.

Useful websites

ollierecycles.com
A fun, interactive site for children about recycling all sorts of materials.

www.recycle-more.co.uk
Games, information and advice about recycling at home and at school.

www.recyclezone.org.uk
Activities, games and information on recycling in general.

www.earthship.com
This site has information and hundreds of pictures showing how earthships are built, as well as finished earthships in many different places.

Index

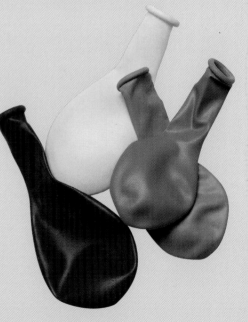